Waiting on the Beloved

The Eucharist as Self-Giving Love

Joyce Ann Zimmerman, CPPS

LTP
LITURGY TRAINING PUBLICATIONS

Nihil Obstat
Deacon David Keene, PHD
Chancellor
Archdiocese of Chicago
August 25, 2023

Imprimatur
Most Rev. Robert G. Casey
Vicar General
Archdiocese of Chicago
August 25, 2023

This book was edited by Timothy A. Johnston. Michael A. Dodd was the production editor, Juan Alberto Castillo was the designer, and Kari Nicholls was the production artist.

Cover art by Linda McCray

28 27 26 25 24 1 2 3 4 5

Printed in the United States of America

Library of Congress Control Number: 2023945046

ISBN: 978-1-61671-778-0

WOB

CONTENTS

ABBREVIATIONS

CCC	*Catechism of the Catholic Church*, 1994
GS	*Gaudium et spes*, Vatican II, "Pastoral Constitution on the Church in the Modern World," 1965
NRSV	New Revised Standard Version, Catholic Edition, 1995
RM	*The Roman Missal*, 2011
SC	*Sacrosanctum concilium*, Vatican II, "Constitution on the Sacred Liturgy," 1963

PREFACE

When I taught Scripture to high school students, during the first class of the semester I would have them take a Bible, turn to the Song of Solomon (or Song of Songs) and begin reading. At first, I heard lots of groans. Then soon the classroom quieted down. Then I could hear only pages turning. Rather rapidly! It doesn't take much to get adolescents turning pages of a love story, even when it is a text with words slightly different from their everyday language. Love speaks volumes, no matter the language. Listen to this Scriptural love language: "Let him kiss me with the kisses of his mouth!" (Song of Solomon 1:2a; NRSV); "Ah, you are beautiful, my beloved, truly lovely" (1:16a); "The voice of my beloved! Look, he comes" (2:8a); "I will seek him whom my soul loves" (3:2b); " . . . when I found him whom my soul loves. I held him, and would not let him go" (3:4ab); "This is my beloved and this is my friend" (5:16b); "I am my beloved's and my beloved is mine" (6:3a); "I am my beloved's, and his desire is for me" (7:10); " . . . for love is strong as death, passion fierce as the grave" (8:6b).

One interpretation of this Scriptural love poem is that it describes the love relationship between God and God's beloved people. God's love for us is surely not a new insight. Both the Old and New Testaments attest to God's great love for us in many passages. The prophet Hosea is another book of the Bible that simply oozes God's love. Listen to God speaking through Hosea in this passage: "When Israel was a child, I loved him. . . . Yet it was I who taught Ephraim to walk, I took them up in my arms. . . . I was to them like those who lift infants to their cheeks" (Hosea 11:1, 3a, 4b). In the face of Israel's infidelity, we can hear—no, we can feel—God's love, God's great desire for intimate union with God's people, God's unfailing and abiding love. It is tempting to measure divine love by our own capacity to give and receive love. But this tendency falls so short of the awe-inspiring reality of God's love for us.

This divine love is extraordinarily expressed with the incarnation, where the Second Person of the Holy Trinity emptied himself of his divinity to assume our humanity (see Philippians 2:6–8). This divine love act ushered in a new commandment, to love one another as God loves us. At that intimate meal Jesus shared with his followers, the Last Supper, Jesus expresses this new commandment clearly: "I give you a new commandment, that you love one another. Just as I have loved you, you also should love one another" (John 13:34). What a command! Our love must be just as Jesus loves us. And how does Jesus love us? With his all! So must our love for one another be with our all.

We sometimes get so focused on Jesus' ministry, death, and resurrection that we forget the significance of the incarnation in itself and its effect on us. Listen to the collect prayer for the Mass during the Day for Christmas: "O God, who wonderfully created the dignity of human nature / and still more wonderfully restored it, / grant, we pray, / that we may share in the divinity of Christ, / who humbled himself to share in our humanity. / Who lives and reigns with you in the unity of the Holy Spirit, God, for ever and ever. Amen." This prayer begins with humanity's very creation: "the dignity of human nature" was established at the beginning of our existence when God created each of us in the divine image (see Genesis 1:27). But God takes one more amazing step: when Jesus assumed his human nature, identifying with us in all things, even death, only excepting sin (see Hebrews 4:15), he made it possible for us to share in God's very own Life, God's divinity. Jesus' humility raises us up to unprecedented Life! Jesus' humility is love made visible. As we open ourselves to love's mystery, we ourselves are to be love made visible.

I am very aware of what a daunting task it is to use words to capture the mystery of divine love seeking us and our response. The only appropriate response in the face of such mystery is waiting on our Beloved. This is not a waiting that implies God is never present to us.

Our waiting on our Beloved is a matter of waiting on ourselves to become ever more deeply aware, responsive, self-emptying, self-giving, seeking, yearning, and expecting. The mystery of divine love challenges us to open ourselves to all the richness and mystery that God offers us. This mystery can be approached from many aspects. In these pages our lens is Eucharist and paschal mystery. Indeed, herein lies the kernel of divine love and its mystery.

Six chapters explore how we wait on the Beloved, with each chapter being divided into a trinity of reflections. After each of the three reflections of each chapter, a pause for reflection and prayer is included. This book is intended for spiritual reading that, hopefully, draws the reader into a quiet communion with the Beloved. Chapter 1 reminds us that God chooses us first, so we must quicken our response to the mystery of divine love. Chapter 2 reflects on God's invitation into the divine Mystery, especially with baptism and our ongoing commitment to live the Gospel. Chapter 3 delves into the continuing self-giving of the risen Christ in the Eucharist, where we are transformed into more perfect members of the Body of Christ. This chapter spills over into Chapter 4 with an exploration into the Self-giving of the Eucharist that invokes the very same self-giving of each of us. Chapters 5 and 6 describe the life and living that flow from embracing the Eucharist as paschal mystery: a life for waiting and living an intimate union with God and each other.

In the first three chapters, we survey God's unfathomable love, which quite frankly needs even more than the words here can possibly express. In the last three chapters the shift is to us and our work in what we do with this gift of divine love. Love flows from the Beloved to those who are loved and then back to the Beloved. Eucharist is the heart of that love. At Eucharist the waiting is over. The Beloved possesses us. We possess the Beloved.

This book has its origins in the unexpected, as I suppose a book addressing the mystery of divine love would. I was sitting at breakfast with a dear friend in February 2018, and somehow the conversation turned to prayer. Three hours later, I was simply in awe of the shared beauty of our conversation. My friend left the table to take care of some things, and all of a sudden, I found myself scribbling on the back of a Sudoku puzzle the outline for this book. Why take over four years to sit down and begin filling out the outline into a book? I found it took me this long to try and grasp the mystery with which I was confronted. How does one capture God's immense love for us? After years of reflecting on this, I'm not sure yet. I know as I sit down to write that it is time, and it will only be a start. I am immensely grateful to my friend for our conversation that morning that seems now long ago, and then for our continued conversations as this book unfolded. She graciously and generously read each chapter, and then we discussed how to make my drafts better. But mostly, I am grateful to her for continually challenging me in my prayer life and my love for the Eucharist. I will be immensely grateful if this book helps others enter into the mystery of waiting on the Beloved.

CHAPTER 1

The Beloved Chooses Us

Especially among young people, certain words catch on and are often repeated that express overwhelming joy, surprise, approval, and so on. For example, in decades past the words were "groovy" and "cool"; then came along "sweet" and "swell." Now "awesome" is the in word. We human beings often have experiences that overtake us with emotion, take us "over the top," that are beyond fully sharing by use of an easy word or expression. Although conveying such experiences to another is difficult, some people still often have a strong impulse to share. We use language that approximates the experience, we repeat ourselves, we become dissatisfied knowing that we just can't get across the depth we wish to convey. But we keep trying! Awesome experiences beg to be shared.

One of the Seven Gifts of the Holy Spirit is "the fear of the Lord" (see Isaiah11:2, Proverbs 1:7, and CCC 1831). Many take the word *fear* at face value, wondering how it can be a gift of the Spirit of God to be frightened of God. But this is not what is meant by this special Gift of the Holy Spirit and the word *fear.* The phrase "fear of the Lord" is often used in Scripture, almost fifty times in the Old Testament and at least twice in the New Testament (see 2 Corinthians 5:11 and Acts 9:31). The meaning here is awe, reverence, loving obedience to God's will. Fear of the Lord is more than an emotion or attitude; rather, it describes our orientation and relationship to God. *Fear* is a word that attempts to describe the superabundance of the mystery of God choosing to relate to us and our response. In a word, our fear of the Lord captures how utterly awesome God is for us.

Who Is This Awesome God?

The more we know God, the more we are able to "fear" God—that is, to have awe, respect, reverence, love, obedience. To know God is far more than an intellectual exercise; it's possible to have knowledge about God and not really know God. Head knowledge is not heart knowledge. Knowing God (head knowledge) is a fruit of encountering God (heart knowledge). We must make ourselves receptive to God's abiding divine Presence to us, which comes in many ways. The more we surrender ourselves to divine Presence and become intimate with God, the more God becomes our Beloved. Only then can we begin to grasp how the Beloved chooses us.

God is called by many names—for example, Creator, Shepherd, Lord, King, Rock, Judge, heavenly Father, Healer, and Savior. Notice how even in Scripture our address to God often discloses attributes of God rather than very much about who God is in the divine Being. Indeed, when Moses asks God, who sends Moses to free God's people, for the name to speak to Pharaoh, God responds with "I AM has sent me to you" (Exodus 3:14). The Hebrew is transliterated as YHWH or Yahweh, the sacred name that devout Jews never pronounce out of reverence for the awesomeness of God.

Known as the Tetragrammaton (four letters), YHWH is thought to derive from the Hebrew verb for "to be." This does give us some insight into who God is—that is, God simply *is*. Awesome! God as a divine Being who always was from the beginning and always will be is difficult for us humans to grasp. Pure Being with no beginning or end is a stunning mystery and very much beyond our human experience. Simple existence, however, does not satisfy us in our quest to know God. Let us take a leap and say, with St. John, that "God is love"

(1 John 4:16b). A caution here: to define God as love is to demand a deeper understanding of love than how it is all too often used in everyday language and living.

Love is not some sugary feeling or petty affectation. It certainly is not a selfish seeking of self-pleasure. No, for our context, love is the depth of being that exists totally for the other, that moves toward a self-giving that is life-giving for us, the beloved of God. Divine love is all this and more and is a model for the way we love one another.

When we think about God, we often move immediately to what God does for us, to divine actions on our behalf. Traditionally, the First Person of the Blessed Trinity (God the Father) is the Creator; the Second Person of the Blessed Trinity (God the Son, Jesus) is the Redeemer; the Third Person of the Blessed Trinity (the Holy Spirit) is the Sanctifier. All of these actions by God benefit us: we are created in God's image (see Genesis 1:27), we are offered salvation by the unsurpassed obedience of Jesus, divine Life is poured forth within us by the indwelling of the Holy Spirit. God has acted from the creation of the first human beings to draw us ever more closely into divine Presence.

There is a beautiful image of God's desire for intimacy with us humans expressed when Adam and Eve were in the Garden of Paradise. Imagine God walking "in the garden at the time of the evening breeze" (Genesis 3:8a) with Adam and Eve. We can easily picture this relaxing encounter. Maybe God would ask Adam and Eve how their naming of creatures was going (see Genesis 2:20), or if what they ate of the trees and vegetation in the Garden was satisfying, or if there was anything else God could do for them to make their time in the Garden even more joyful and happy. Or maybe Adam and Eve would ask God if there would be any new and interesting animal created, or why the trees bore more fruit than they could possibly eat, or how they could please God even more. Perhaps God walked between Adam and Eve, holding their hands in loving embrace. Adam and Eve had it all!

So what did they do? They became dissatisfied with their idyllic life and wanted even more. They succumbed to the serpent's temptation. Adam and Eve's fall involved far more than simple disobedience of God's command not to eat "of the tree of the knowledge of good and evil" (see Genesis 2:15). The Hebrew text has an interesting play on the word *knowledge*. The Hebrew root for the word is used in an experiential, relational way. The serpent was wily, tempting Adam and Eve at the heart of their being. Knowledge of good and evil would make them gods. So they ate, and lost everything. Adam and Eve's sin was really dissatisfaction with who God created them to be and all the good they had been given freely by God. They chose to eat of the forbidden fruit, thinking that disobedience would make them to be gods. Here is the irony of this account: Adam and Eve lost Paradise; they lost their innocence; they became ashamed of who they were. But God continues to choose them and us. And in Christ Jesus, we are given what Adam and Eve lost: a share in God's divine Life (more about this in a later chapter). One would think that after Adam and Eve's heinous act, God would give up on us humans. But no—God continues to choose us, even when we fail.

The entire Old Testament is a narrative of God's awesome fidelity, of God's faithfully choosing God's beloved people despite their infidelity, of the people's continually choosing alien ways. God sends prophets to remind the people of their covenant with God and to call them back to loving, covenantal fidelity. Reminding the people that they had strayed from God was not an easy task for the prophets. It is far easier to stray and go our own way than remain faithful to God's commands. God's true prophets never swerved from what God told them to say to the people. For this, the prophets suffered.

We can learn much from the prophet Jeremiah. First, God chose Jeremiah: "Before I formed you in the womb I knew you, and before you were born I consecrated you; I appointed you a prophet to the nations" (Jeremiah 1:5). Jeremiah's prophetic task was to plead with Israel to repent of their infidelity, to turn from the false gods they had embraced. They did not listen. Jeremiah suffers and expresses his lament to God: he decries ever being born, he is cursed by others, and he could no longer make merry with his friends, who shun him (see Jeremiah 15:10, 12). Jeremiah has every right to complain, for he is persecuted (see Jeremiah 20), imprisoned (see Jeremiah 37), thrown into a cistern to die (see Jeremiah 38), and taken to Egypt by the remnant Israelites against God's command (see Jeremiah 42–43); tradition has it that Jeremiah was stoned to death in Egypt. Being chosen by God is awesome, but it carries with it challenges to loving, covenantal fidelity.

Who is this awesome God? The One who creates, loves, enters into covenantal relationship with God's beloved People. The One who seemingly never tires of relenting of punishment when we stray, but always calls us back into intimate relationship. The One who chooses us to make the divine Presence known. The One who chooses to be in relationship with us in spite of our shortsighted infidelity. Who is this awesome God who seems to grasp us at all costs? This awesome God is the God who is love.

It is difficult for us to grasp a Being who is pure love. But that is who God is. And because God is pure love, God is pure relationship. Called the *immanent* Trinity, God in Godself is a Self-giving Being defined by innate love. Above, we said love is the depth of being that exists totally for the other; love moves toward a self-giving that is life-giving for the beloved. God's love is so dynamic that it is three divine Persons. Imagine: a Self-giving so total as to generate another distinct Person, each proceeding One from the Other. Each of the three Persons of the Holy Trinity is so loving and so Self-giving that they remain one God while maintaining their distinctiveness as Persons (see CCC, 253–255).

We human beings are sensate individuals; we perceive through our senses. It is most difficult for us to imagine pure spirit. This is one reason why grasping who God is in Godself is so difficult. Most of us can visualize God as Father because creation reflects good fathers, a familiar relationship for us humans. Jesus is even easier for us to visualize because this divine Son took on our very flesh. The Holy Spirit is the most difficult, because there is no relational equivalent such as Father or Son.

Traditionally, the Holy Spirit has been visualized as a dove, a gentle bird associated with peace. A dove returned to Noah with an olive branch in its beak to symbolize that the chaotic rains have ended (see Genesis 8:11), thus bringing peace, forgiveness, and the beginning of new life on earth. A dove appeared at Jesus' baptism to announce his identity as the beloved Son (see Matthew 3:16; also Mark 1:10 and Luke 3:22).

A non-Scriptural, legendary symbol for the Holy Spirit cherished by the ancient Celtic people is a wild goose. In contrast to the gentleness of a dove, a wild goose is unpredictable, rambunctious, loud, cannot be contained, and bites when threatened. The symbol of the wild goose reminds us that the Holy Spirit can surprise us, upset our plans, and nudge us toward new life.

Another image of the Holy Spirit is the tongues of fire that descended upon the gathered disciples on the day of Pentecost, after the ascension of the risen Christ into heaven (see Acts 2:3). As the tongues of fire divided and settled over each person present, they were all filled with the Holy Spirit. Yet another image for the Holy Spirit is breath (Hebrew: *rûah*). We pretty much take breathing for granted; we inhale and exhale automatically. Without taking in oxygen, we do not live very long. Anyone who has had a serious choking or near-drowning experience knows what it is like to fight for breath, for life. The Spirit is our breath of divine Life. Here is what Psalm 104 has to say about breath, spirit, and life: "When you take away [the creatures'] breath, they die and return to their dust. When you send forth your spirit [breath], they are created" (vv. 29b–30a). It may be a good prayer practice to pause at times during the day, become aware of our breathing, and recognize the Breath of God within us. The Spirit is the love shared between the Father and Son and is God's breath of Life dwelling within us. The images of dove, fire, and breath are inanimate, and perhaps not as easily relatable as personal images. Nonetheless, the Spirit is a divine Person, an awesome Presence of God.

Let us consider yet one more view about who this awesome God is. The Greek term *perichoresis* has been used to describe the dynamic of God's inner Self since about the sixth century. It basically means "to come or dance around." Our English word *choreography* is derived from this Greek term. It tickles the imagination to think of the three Persons of the Holy Trinity as dance partners. Dancing is lively and relational. To dance with someone is to be near, to be in step, to be in unity. This is one reason why dancing is so prevalent at wedding receptions, those beautiful celebrations of love. And especially thought-provoking is the father-daughter (or mother-son) first dance. The beautiful and close relationship of parent-child is remembered and shared as fresh love is expressed in the newlyweds. The *perichoresis* of the Trinity describes the dynamic love interpenetration of the three Persons of the Holy Trinity. This interpenetration is so energetic as to be Life-giving. God is not a static idol someplace in the sky. God is a wholly relational Being in and of Self who is loving and Life-giving. How awesome it is that God is so dynamic! so active! so Self-giving!

Reflective and Prayerful Interlude

- **God is awesome for me in these ways . . .**
- **Other names or images for God meaningful to me are . . .**
- **God is always faithful to me, and so I . . .**
- **For me, God is . . .**

How Does This Awesome God Choose Us?

We often think of the notion of "call" as limited to a few "special" people in the Church who are priests or religious sisters and brothers. While certainly these ministers of the Church have a vocation, a call from God to these particular ways of living, it is good to remind ourselves that each of us has a call from God; this is how God chooses us. Scripture is full of call narratives. Probably one of the most familiar to us is the call of Saul, who had been persecuting the Church. While on the way to Damascus to gather Christians to bring them bound back to Jerusalem (Acts 9), God intervenes with a call: "But get up and enter the city, and you will be told what you are to do" (Acts 9:6). Paul heard the call, responded to the call, and became the great evangelizer of the Gentiles.

Call narratives of the prophets often share a similar pattern of elements. Let us consider the call of Moses (see Exodus 3:1–15). Moses' call comes amid his daily task of tending the sheep of his father-in-law. His call unfolds in six movements.

1. There is a *theophany* (divine appearance) on "Horeb, the mountain of God": an angel appears in a burning bush that is not consumed. Naturally, Moses is quite interested in this phenomenon and turns aside to see what is happening. Moses, probably without realizing it, turns toward God with an attitude of readiness. To hear God calling or choosing us, we must eagerly be open to God's Presence.

2. God speaks an introductory word to Moses; in fact, God addresses Moses by name not once, but twice. In Scriptural poetry, repetition is an indication of importance, significance. The encounter between God and Moses is no ordinary encounter; something singular is about to take place. Moses responds readily: "Here I am." Then God reveals the divine Self, and Moses hides his face, for in that culture to see God was to die.

3. God then commissions Moses to go to Pharaoh to release the enslaved people of Israel. This is the reason for the call.

4. Naturally, Moses is appalled: "Who am I that I should go to Pharaoh, and bring the Israelites out of Egypt?" This question underscores the real choice we have in being called by God for a particular mission, but also the utter surprise we experience with a call from God. Moses is asking God for some clarification and assurance.

5. God is not offended by Moses' question but is patient and reassures Moses with the promise that God will be with Moses. When God calls, God remains with us to fulfill the mission requested. We are never alone when God chooses us.

6. God offers a sign of the divine election and mission: "I will be with you," and when Moses' mission is complete the Israelites will worship God on the very mountain where this divine-human exchange has occurred.

Not all call narratives so clearly include these six movements. For example, the call of Isaiah is similar to Moses', but there are notable differences (see Isaiah 6:1–13). There is a lovely spontaneity in Isaiah's call. Theophany: Isaiah is in the temple and sees "the Lord sitting on the throne, high and lofty." While Moses seems to show deference to God, Isaiah seems to acknowledge God's greatness. The introductory words are not spoken to Isaiah, nor is Isaiah called by name as was Moses, but the introductory words are spoken by the Seraph angels attending the Lord: "Holy, holy, holy is the LORD of hosts; the whole earth is full of his glory." Only with the commissioning does God speak directly to Isaiah, but with a question: "Whom shall I send, and who will go for us?" Again, Isaiah has a choice. God does not force on us a response to a call; God utterly respects our freedom. Isaiah's objection comes before God's invitation to mission, when Isaiah laments that he is "a man of unclean lips." God does not choose perfect people for a mission; rather, God reassures Isaiah (and us) by sending "one of the seraphs . . . holding a live coal . . . [and touching] . . . [his] mouth with it," which cleansed Isaiah. With this reassurance, Isaiah readily responds "Here am I; send me!" The commission is given: "Go and say to this people"; Isaiah is sent to be a prophet—the sign is that Isaiah's words are not his own, but God tells Isaiah the words to speak to the people.

God's call does not usually come to us in such extraordinary ways. Sometimes it comes through the intervention of another; for example, Peter's call came through Andrew (see John 1:40–42) and Nathanael's call came through Philip (see John 1:43ff). Jesus' disciples were ordinary people going about their everyday labors (such as fishermen and tax collectors). We have one example of someone who walked away from Jesus' call (see Mark 10:17–31). A rich young man (not named!) approaches Jesus, kneels before him, and asks what he must do to "inherit eternal life." Jesus responds by telling him to live the commandments as he has been taught. But the rich man pushes Jesus to say more. Here is where it got difficult for the rich young man, for Jesus told him to "Go, sell what you own, and give the money to the poor, and you will have treasure in heaven; then come, follow me." Before issuing this dying-to-self call, Jesus "look[ed] at him, [and] loved him." Where was that rich young man's heart? How could he refuse Jesus' look and love? Obviously, his wealth was more important to him than committing himself to Jesus by following him. This is certainly a heart-rending wake-up call for us: Is there anything in our lives more important than following Jesus faithfully? If so, then we are like the rich young man who walked away from Jesus' look and love. How could we ever do that?

What keeps us from becoming the rich young man is holding Jesus at the center of our heart and life. Only then can we hear the call of God and be faithful to the mission on which we are sent. We might hear God's call through others, as did some of the apostles. We hear God's call in the midst of fulfilling our everyday obligations. Sometimes the call prompts us to do something. Occasionally it is an "itch" or urge that keeps coming back. At other times God's call might come during liturgy or our personal prayer. However a call comes, we need to take it seriously, examine if it is truly from God, and pray for the willingness to exercise our freedom to say yes.

There are different calls in our lives. For example, God's invitation might determine our life's overall direction, and this is how we often think of vocation—such as to the priesthood, religious life, married state, or single state. But besides this kind of invitation, God continues to call us to mission as we grow and our life circumstances change. A very good woman had a high-paying job in industry. For several years she struggled with feeling a call from God to let go and become a full-time parish minister, with a salary half as much as she earned before. She had a supportive husband and so felt she could answer the call. Now she says she cannot imagine doing anything else or being any happier, in spite of the challenges of parish ministry. Another person, after retirement, heard God calling and became involved at both parish and diocesan levels in social justice causes. Someone else, after he became seriously ill and could no longer hold a paying position, heard God's call to take up a prayer ministry for peace in the world.

God's call can be to fulfill a rather visible and far-reaching mission, or it might be to fulfill a simple request that comes our way unexpectedly. Answering God's call isn't always life-changing, nor is it always a difficult challenge. Nonetheless, God chooses to call us to cooperate in God's desire for us to come to salvation, to be holy, to be friends with God and each other. In Jesus' discourse at the Last Supper, he reminds us, "I have called you friends. . . . You did not choose me but I chose you" (John 15:15b, 16a).

God chooses us because God cherishes us from the very beginning of our lives; God knows us better than we know ourselves: "O Lord, you have searched me and known me. / You know when I sit down and rise up; / you discern my thoughts from far away" (Psalm 139:1–2). Later in this psalm we are told that God knows us intimately because it was God "who formed / my inward parts; / you knit me together in my mother's womb" (Psalm 139:13). No wonder the psalmist exclaimed, "I praise you, for I am fearfully and wonderfully made" (Psalm 139:14a)! In our creation and call God bestows upon us an astounding dignity!

To hear the many and diverse calls God issues, we must be people who are open to God, be willing to surrender ourselves to do what God invites for the sake of others, and be people of prayer who take time daily to place ourselves in divine Presence, encounter God, and listen with our hearts open and willing. And perhaps take time to be grateful that God chooses us!

Reflective and Prayerful Interlude

- **God has called me to . . .**
- **Discernment of God's call happens to me when I . . .**
- **I have experienced these movements of God's call in my life . . .**
    - **Awareness of God's Presence (*theophany*)**
    - **Introductory word**
    - **Commission**
    - **Objection**
    - **Reassurance**
    - **Sign**
- **I thank God for calling me to . . .**

Why Does This Awesome God Choose Us?

That is a really good question! In a moment of boldness, we might say because we are lovable. Really? How so?

God's intent in creating us in the divine image was to give us everything possible to make us happy. Before the Fall there was no death, no sickness, no work. What a great life! Having loved us into existence, and choosing to relate to us intimately in friendship, God bestowed upon us an inherent dignity (Latin: *dignitas*, worthy). Just by living, by being, we have a worthiness unequalled in the rest of creation: "Man occupies a unique place in creation" (CCC, 355). We have a special value unique to us because we alone are created in God's image. God chooses us because we are worthy of divine election. Not because of anything we do or accomplish, but simply because God chooses to make us in the divine image: "Being in the image of God the human individual possesses the dignity of a person, who is not just something, but someone" (CCC, 357). In a sense, when God chooses us, God chooses Self.

It is sad indeed when we humans do not live in a dignified way or respect the dignity of all other human beings. It is as though we lose sight of our inherent self-worth. We lose sight of the God-given gift of being able to know and love God our Creator (GS, 12). Being able to know and love is being able to choose. God chooses us; we choose God. God's invitation is compelling; our response is gratifying. Each of us has a call from God to be who we were created to be. This call is a gift that demands a wholehearted response from us.

Another motive for God's choosing us is that God desires that we humans be partners in God's saving work. How awesome is that! There is a curious admission that St. Paul makes in his letter to the Colossians: "In my flesh I am completing what is lacking in Christ's afflictions for the sake of his body, that is, the church" (Colossians 1:24). Obviously, nothing is "lacking" in Christ's saving ministry; nothing can be added to the fruits of the passion, death, and resurrection of Christ for all people at all times. What could Paul possibly mean here? Carefully reading the passage suggests that the "lack" is not in Christ's saving act itself, but in our participating in and internalizing it for ourselves. Our whole life is a journey into the mystery of Christ. Often, we are reminded that we unite our own sufferings with those of Christ. And, as Paul intimates, not just for suffering's sake, but for the sake of the Body of Christ, the Church. In our own suffering, our own dying to self, we grow more Christ-like and witness the Gospel to others. We are the mediators (priests by the dignity of our baptism) today who make known Christ's Good News.

God chooses us as a way to relate to us and in turn calls us to be in intimate relationship with God. As divine Persons, God communicates Self to us. By choosing us, God opens the divine Being to us. Our saying yes to God's call is our way of opening ourselves to God's Presence, God's will, God's friendship. It is awesome indeed to reflect on God's choosing us. With God choosing us, the waiting is over. The Beloved possesses us. We possess the Beloved.

Reflective and Prayerful Interlude

- I recognize my dignity when . . .
- I recognize the dignity of others when . . .
- God is awesome for choosing me in that . . .
- The gifts I have to offer God and others are . . .
- I marvel that God chooses me for God's work because . . .

CHAPTER 2

The Beloved Invites Us

The Beloved invites us to what? Well, we are invited to many divine encounters, to surprising life-giving opportunities, to new expressions of love and fidelity. The Beloved chooses us for a life of responding to divine invitations. In a sense, then, all our life is a matter of answering God's overtures. When we let go and open our hearts, we allow ourselves to be guided on the journey of life by God's impulses and will. Our life then bears fruit in many and unexpected ways, not least of which is a deep joy and happiness that affirms that all is well. Even in the face of trials and disappointments and sometimes failures, God is always with us, teaching us how to walk the journey of life.

The most perfect invitation God issues is to be united with the divine Being. The amazing reality of this invitation is that we don't have to wait until our biological death to be united with God. Because Jesus became incarnate, we already have an open door to union with God. When Jesus passed from this mortal life to risen Life, he did not then ascend to heaven saying, "Bye, bye, I've made it, now you're on your own." Heavens no! The disciples were not to stand there "looking up toward heaven" (Acts 1:11), as if their yearning for him would bring Jesus back down to earth. At the ascension, Jesus promised his Spirit, his risen Presence, would descend upon the disciples (see Acts 1:8). With the coming of the Holy Spirit, Jesus' saving mystery is entrusted to us to continue his preaching and teaching, his love and compassion, his mercy and forgiveness.

We can only continue Jesus' saving mission by participating in the paschal mystery—the mystery of his dying and rising. We need to shift our perspective on the paschal mystery beyond what happened to Jesus over two millennia ago, beyond a theological concept, beyond a mystery to be embraced only by a special few holy people. We ourselves are immersed in the paschal mystery at our baptism. Baptism plunges us into the dying and rising mystery of the risen Christ, which defines who we are as his followers and governs how we follow. In other words, baptism confers both an identity and a mission. This is the Christian call. Our baptismal yes is to be the Presence of the risen Christ for others. Our baptismal yes marks us very personally for Christ.

Dying Is Not All Bad

Jesus taught us the perfect prayer, the Our Father. The struggle with praying such a familiar prayer is that we do not really think about what we are saying; we do not think about the words and implications of our prayer. In the Our Father we pray "thy will be done on earth as it is in heaven." It is the "as" word that is so challenging! We know that those in heaven do God's will perfectly. Why? Because they are in perfect union with God, the Beloved. But we who haven't passed from this life to the next are not yet in perfect union with the Beloved; our journey toward perfection is not over yet. So when we pray these words of the Our Father, we are not setting ourselves up for failure, but rather expressing our desire to complete the journey faithfully.

Just before we pray these words about God's will being done, we ask that God's kingdom come. When God's will *is* done on earth, God's kingdom *is* present. God's kingdom is not a spatial, physical place but rather a realm of divine Presence. When we do God's will, God is present. It really is that simple. But sometimes doing God's will is a real challenge. It is faith that helps us meet this challenge.

Faith is not simply adherence to a set of beliefs or doctrines. Faith is actually a verb, an action. Consider the people of faith whom we admire and imitate. Abraham immediately comes to mind. Like Moses and Isaiah, whom we considered above, Abraham had a call from God: "Go from your country and your kindred and your father's house to the land that I will show you" (Genesis 12:1). In Abraham's call we do not have the objections or assurances or signs that we often see in other call narratives. It appears all that is skipped over. In the face of God's call and promises, the account simply says, "So Abram went" (Genesis 12:4). Such faith! Abraham gets up and journeys into an unknown land. Abraham says yes to God seemingly without questioning. Abraham's unmitigated yes is his expression of faith in a God who will ask even more of him.

Later in the narrative, God makes a covenant with Abraham, and his name is changed from *Abram*, meaning something like "exalted father," to *Abraham*, meaning "the ancestor of a multitude of nations" (Genesis 17:4–5). In Scripture, a name change often means a mission change; for example, Simon becomes Peter, the foundational "rock" of the Church; Saul becomes known by his Latin name, Paul, who no longer persecutes Christians but becomes the apostle to the Gentiles. Armed with God's covenant and promises, Abraham continues to say yes to God. But the real test of his faith comes when God commands Abraham to sacrifice Isaac, the son of his and Sarah's old age (see Genesis 22). Imagine saying yes to sacrificing one's own beloved son! Because of Abraham's faith, Isaac is spared.

As in the patriarch Abraham's life, saying yes to God today might make some heavy demands on us. Our yes to God's invitation is not better or more pleasing to God the more difficult something is for us. No, the issue here is that we are called to say yes to God many times in our daily living, and sometimes the yes is more demanding, sometimes less so. No matter how demanding, our yes will bear fruit for the kingdom. The key is the yes. We said above that we do not have to wait until our biological death to be united with God. Nor do we have to wait until our biological death to die with Christ. All we need to do is surrender to Gospel living with a wholehearted yes.

St. Paul tells us what the basis of this surrender must be: "Do you not know that all of us who have been baptized into Christ Jesus were baptized into his death? (Romans 6:3). We are called to crucify ourselves with Jesus. To grasp this more practically—after all, baptism does not call us literally to be crucified! If so, how many would choose to be baptized?—we are called to surrender ourselves to a yes stance, a faith action in the very way we live each and every day. Realistically speaking, this means we must be willing to die to ourselves, to die to our own desires especially when they are not in line with Gospel living, to die to anything at all that removes us from God's Presence.

It does not make sense to think that Jesus' Father sent him to take on human flesh and dwell among us just to suffer and die. Jesus came among us to reveal his Father's love for us and desire to be one with us. Jesus and his Father are one (see John 10:30); as we identify more perfectly with Jesus through dying to self for the good of others, we are united in Jesus with his Father. Jesus was handed over to the Roman authorities to be crucified because he was utterly faithful to doing his Father's will in all things, even when it provoked some of the Jewish leadership (see CCC, 572). The only way to be in union with God is through dying to self. Yes, sometimes we might provoke others by our Gospel living. Like Jesus we may at times be ridiculed, shunned, questioned. But also like Jesus, we must choose to die to self. That is the only way to enter the mystery of salvation.

Many opportunities occur each day to die to self and be in union with the risen Christ's saving mystery. Sometimes these daily "dyings" are more consequential—for example, when we resist the temptation to go against God's will because we want to put our desires ahead of God's will. Most of the time, though, we choose to die to self in all the myriad small ways of caring for and loving others, being attentive to all others as was Jesus. Most of the time we are not even aware of dying to self for the sake of others. This is especially true when we develop loving habits that become the distinctive way we live and express ourselves.

We probably do not think that a kind smile to the cashier at the grocery store along with a sincere thank you is dying to self. After all, it really does not cost us anything, does it? Actually, it does! This simple act does cost us a bit of ourselves being given over to another. That is why such simple gestures can be so profound. Smiling at another is relational, and striving for a holy relationship is a holy act of faith.

Perhaps a bit more demanding, dying to self might come in the form of how we approach disagreements. So much of our lives (family, church, society) are divided. These divisions can even break down or destroy relationships. Dying to self does not mean that we must always agree with everything another says. It does mean that the way we disagree must be accompanied by charity toward the other. To enter into a charitably-driven disagreement with another means that we must be open to the other, listen with our heart, and perhaps even be willing to change and let go of our own position. Growth can occur in most unusual circumstances, sometimes when we least expect it. Dying to self, even in small and seemingly insignificant ways, always leads us along our journey of growing in our relationship with the risen Christ.

Conceivably the most consequential way we die to ourselves is by being faithful to our baptismal commitment to live as Christ lived. Gospel living costs because it obliges us to keep Christ at the center of our heart and life. This means that we do not make choices based on our own wants and desires, but solely on whether the choice before us images the Presence of the risen Christ for others. Dying to self is not a matter of never being good to ourselves. When we have worked hard to live the Gospel on a particular day, treating ourselves to something we like (maybe chocolate!) or enjoy (maybe going for a leisurely walk in a beautiful park) or need (maybe taking a nap) can fortify us for the next day's dying-to-self challenges. Dying to self does mean that we strive in all things to fall more deeply in love with our Beloved by keeping the good of the other always before us.

When we begin paying attention to how many opportunities present themselves each day for dying to self, for being Christ-like for others, we might be surprised. As we grow along our journey into Christ, we become more aware of opportunities to die to self that we would not have even noticed the day or month or year before. If we cannot die to ourselves in the small demands, we diminish our ability to choose to die to ourselves in the things that matter the most. Dying to self is a way of baptismal living.

Dying is not all bad because it always leads to a more caring, compassionate, and loving self. Even on the cross Jesus was reaching out to another when he told the Good Thief, "Today you will be with me in Paradise" (Luke 23:43). Even in the midst of extreme pain and suffering, Jesus is always the caring One. We do not need to be crucified, in great pain and suffering, or be at the point of death to die to self. No, dying to self asks that we keep Jesus' life and ministry ever before us, guiding us to choose the good for ourselves and others. No, dying is not all bad because it ultimately leads to risen Life.

Reflective and Prayerful Interlude

- **Today I died to myself in these ways . . .**
- **When I die to myself, I experience . . .**
- **What helps me to choose dying to self is . . .**
- **I am more aware of opportunities to die to self when I . . .**

Rising Is All Good

The paschal mystery "stands at the center of the Good News that the apostles, and the Church following them, are to proclaim to the world" (CCC, 571). Jesus died on the cross once and for all and passed to his rightful place at the right hand of God. This paschal event is not forever relegated to the past. It lives on in us in our own daily living. But the cross—that is, dying to self—is only one dimension of the paschal mystery. Rising to new Life is the other side of dying.

Someone once said, "I've got the dying part of the mystery down pat; when does the rising happen?" That is a fair enough question, but really misleading because it exposes a linear, chronological approach to the paschal mystery: if we choose to die to self, then we rise to new Life. While the dying always includes the rising, it is not a matter of one following the other. It is more that, as we learn to die to self, we more perfectly identify ourselves with the risen Christ and more perfectly reflect his Presence to others, his risen Life. Hence, in the very dying is the rising because we become more intimately united with our Beloved. We cannot share in Christ's risen Life if we do not share in his death by dying to ourselves.

Here is a very simple example of an experience of rising to new Life. Maybe we have an elderly relative who is in a care center. Anyone who has ever walked the halls in these institutions can readily recognize that there are many lonely people living in them. But our lives are busy. At the end of our day or week we are tired. We just want to rest. Yet we feel a responsibility not to abandon our relative, a responsibility felt even more acutely if the relative is a close one such as a parent. So we choose to make the effort to visit. No doubt we are met with a grateful smile. Often the only effort we need to make in the visit is to be present and to listen. The more we surrender ourselves to the other's need, the more enjoyable is the visit. Nevertheless, here is the twist of irony: the other might be overjoyed at our taking the time to be present, but as we leave, we become aware of a quiet, inner joy we ourselves feel. Our effort to make another person happy results in our own happiness growing. This is how dying to self and rising to new Life play out in so many ways.

As we become more aware of the blessings of risen Life gifted to us, we might notice that we develop grateful hearts. While dying to self is a choice we make, the new Life given us is pure gift from God. We do not die in order to receive new Life. The paschal mystery is not about getting something or bargaining with God. Rather, when we die to self the Beloved chooses to gift us with Life. This gift of new Life moves us to a thankful heart. Gratitude is a kind of relationship. It arises with gift exchange, but effects a self-exchange. So living the paschal mystery continually renews our relationship with God, a relationship that inspires awesome gratitude.

We live in chronological, counting, clock time so much that we take it for granted. But when we live the paschal mystery, clock time is not important. Yes, our choosing to die to self takes place in chronological time. But the process of dying leading to rising takes place in a different kind of time. Greek has two words for time: *chronos* and *kairos.*

First is *chronos*, which is clock time, passing time, counting time. We need *chronos* to live together as human beings or not much would get done, certainly not much done together. *Chronos* gets us to work or school or Mass on time, enables us to sit down together for a meal, assists us in meeting friends and having a good time. Life would be chaotic without *chronos.* As important as this time is, another time helps us enter more easily and deeply into the dying-rising dynamic of the paschal mystery.

The second Greek word for time is *kairos.* This time has no duration. It is described as a point in time (do not think second or minute or hour or day or month or year or century, etc.) filled with meaning, a critical point in time, an opportune time. *Kairo*s completely takes over our awareness. This kind of time is the goal of mindfulness or meditation or contemplation. In *kairos* the moment is all there is. We have all had experiences of this kind of time. Sometimes we are at a celebration that is so joyful and meaningful that we lose all track of time; we are just there. Sometimes we are reading a mystery novel and turn the pages so quickly that pretty soon it is hours past our bedtime. People in love, embraced in the presence of each other, always seem to be in *kairos* time.

Jesus announced the coming of God's kingdom: "The time [Greek text: *kairos*] is fulfilled, and the kingdom of God has come near" (Mark 1:15). *Kairos* is the time in which God acts. It is the time when we encounter eternity. Rising to new Life is all good in that it is a meeting of now and eternity, of earth and heaven. It is God's time gifted to us. Though dying to self takes (sometimes great) effort on our part, rising to new Life is all God's work. It is a human-divine encounter that draws us closer to God and strengthens our resolve to do God's will.

God chooses us, and we must choose God. God invites us into the mystery of the Son's dying and rising, and we must choose to live the mystery. Rising to new Life is all good. This rising offers us a new identity and mission.

Reflective and Prayerful Interlude

- **I experience God's gift of Life to me when . . .**
- **I find it easiest to experience both dying and rising when . . .**
- **I surrender to God's Presence and enter into *kairos* time easiest by . . .**
- **My love for God and others unfolds in *kairos* time when . . .**

Baptism Is an Awesome Extravagance

Many of us were baptized as infants and, obviously, have no recollection of the ritual. It happened "back then." We celebrate birthdays, but few celebrate baptismal days. Baptism is recognized to be more or less an entry into the Church and a certain way of living particular obligations, but not much more. Yet this hardly captures the real import of baptism. When we are baptized, God is awesomely extravagant toward us.

The New Testament offers two complementary approaches to baptism. St. Paul talks about being plunged (the root meaning of *baptism* is to be plunged) into the baptismal waters and dying to self to be raised to new Life in him (see Romans 6:3–5). Paul is teaching that the baptismal waters cause a death to the old self, the sinful self, the self that is alienated from God. The baptismal waters are the "tomb" (this is widespread imagery now) that begets new life. The revised baptismal rite encourages an ample use of water at baptism, even supports immersion or submersion. For many practical reasons it is not always possible to immerse or submerge the one to be baptized into the water. But this fuller sign certainly conveys the dying to the old self that happens. So if the old self dies, who rises from the waters? A new self now infused with the risen Life of Christ. This new self boasts of a new identity, one who is now a member of Christ's Body. As members of Christ's Body, we share the same risen Life in Christ. Baptism invites us into the mystery of Christ. We are gifted with God's very Life, with the indwelling of the Holy Spirit, and are charged with the very mission of the One whom we have become: we are to preach the Gospel by living the Gospel. At baptism God's extravagance is unveiled in the new identity we are given as members of the Body of Christ.

The other New Testament approach to baptism is expressed in the conversation between the Pharisee Nicodemus and Jesus (see John 3). What an interesting conversation! Nicodemus has been meeting secretly with Jesus to learn more about what he is teaching. Immediately, Jesus throws out a shocking statement: "Very truly, I tell you, no one can see the kingdom of God without being born from above" (John 3:3). Nicodemus takes Jesus' statement literally, and exclaims "How can anyone be born after having grown old? Can one enter a second time into the mother's womb and be born?" (John 3:4). Here the emphasis is on a birth into new Life. Jesus goes on to explain that we are "being born of water and the Spirit" (John 3:5). At baptism, God's extravagance is unveiled by a new birth into God's Spirit.

Both approaches to baptism, as tomb and womb, invite us into the mystery of Christ. Both emphasize the new Life God gratuitously gives us. Both emphasize an incorporation into Christ and the Spirit that sets us on a new journey. Baptism is far more than a ritual ceremony. The ritual is the outward sign of a new identity and mission that we receive when we say yes to our baptismal commitment. This yes is not a single utterance; it is a yes that we say (hopefully) every day of our lives, every day that we choose to die to ourselves for the sake of others, every day that we witness to the new identity we have been given as members of the Body of Christ. Baptism is an ongoing life in the Spirit. Baptism initiates God's extravagance toward us. The invitation to live the baptismal life shapes who we are individually and together; it shapes how we love one another, why we choose this way of living. With God's invitation, the waiting is over. The Beloved possesses us. We possess the Beloved.

Reflective and Prayerful Interlude

- **God's extravagance toward me prompts gratitude in that . . .**
- **I could better relate my yes to dying to self to my baptismal promises if I would . . .**
- **The images of "tomb and womb" help me to understand baptism as . . .**
- **I am aware of the meaning of my baptism when . . .**

CHAPTER 3

Eucharist Transforms Us

Toys come and go, but some seem to endure over decades. Hula-Hoops came out in 1958, and they are still around; Barbie dolls came out in 1959 and are just as popular as ever, albeit in new styles; Etch A Sketch was introduced in 1960 and, although a bit fancier and more expensive than four decades ago, is still available. Among the more interesting toys in terms of challenge are Transformers, which came out in 1984 and are still popular because of the current sci-fi film series launched in 2007. Transformers allow the child to move and shape the toy into new looks or new creations (for example, the two Mini-Cassette warriors, Ravage and Raindance, become a panther and a jet, and Bumblebee transforms into a VW beetle). Something similar happens to us at the Eucharistic celebration, with even more staying power than toys.

Transformation is something we probably do not think about with respect to what happens at Mass. Yes, we well know there is a change of the bread and wine into the very Body and Blood of the risen Christ. On the other hand, how many of us think in terms of Eucharist as also bringing about a change in us, also transforming us? This is a profound part of the mystery into which we are invited by the Beloved. We pray in the Prayer after Communion of the Twenty-Seventh Sunday in Ordinary Time, “Grant us, almighty God, / that we may be refreshed and nourished / by the Sacrament which we have received, / so as to be transformed into what we consume. / Through Christ our Lord. Amen” (RM).

Transformed by the Beloved

The things we do at Mass, as well as the Mass prayers themselves, are so helpful in drawing us into the mystery of what is taking place during the Eucharistic celebration. For us to enter more deeply into the mystery, however, we must give ourselves over to what is taking place; we must surrender ourselves to the Eucharistic action and unite ourselves with the risen Christ, who is so lavishly giving himself to us at this time and in this place. In this way we give ourselves to Christ and to each other as well. In this conscious surrender we express who we are and who we are becoming: the Body of Christ united with its Head. More than once during the Eucharistic liturgy we are reminded of who we are and who we are becoming. Nevertheless, to be transformed requires that we be willing to give ourselves over to God’s action within us. And sometimes God’s action within us takes a leap of faith to allow God to do as God chooses with us, especially when God’s answer to our prayers is not what we expect or seems too difficult. We may be tempted to reject God’s answer. Nonetheless, God’s action always unfolds in awesome ways.

We may take for granted the presentation of the gifts that moves us from the Liturgy of the Word into the Liturgy of the Eucharist, but this action is significant. Preferably the gifts are brought through the congregation to the altar (usually from the entrance of the church forward to the altar), symbolizing that the gifts are from the members of the assembly: “for through your goodness we have received / the bread we offer you . . . for through your goodness we have received / the wine we offer you” (“The Order of Mass,” RM, 23, 25). The mystery reveals even more. Not only the gifts of bread and wine are placed on the altar to be offered, but we ourselves are placed on the altar. By our surrender to the action, we ourselves are also offered as gift.

The Prayer over the Offerings sometimes reminds us of the transformation that takes place with the gifts. In even stronger language, some of these prayers expressly state that an exchange takes place, that the gifts (and we) become something new. For example, from the Twentieth Sunday in Ordinary Time: "Receive our oblation, O Lord, / by which is brought about a glorious exchange, / that by offering what you have given, / we may merit to receive your very self. / Through Christ our Lord" (RM). Amazing: we have gifts to offer only because God has given them to us first. All we have and all we are is a love-gift from the Beloved. In the offering of our humble gifts and ourselves we become worthy to receive the greatest Gift God offers us: the very Body and Blood of the divine, risen Son. God takes these gifts and changes them; the gifts *and* we become that "glorious exchange."

With the revision of the Roman Rite after the Second Vatican Council, we have a richness of the mystery we celebrate that ought not to be missed. We now hear quite clearly how the Holy Spirit is active and present in the transformation that happens with the gifts. With slightly different words, almost all the Eucharistic Prayers approved for use include calling down the Holy Spirit upon the gifts "so that they may become for us / the Body and ✠ Blood of our Lord Jesus Christ" ("Eucharistic Prayer II," RM, 101; the invocation of the Holy Spirit is called an *epiclesis*). It is clear that the gifts are transformed by the power of the Holy Spirit. The Spirit is the Agent of change. But even more happens.

We also pray "that, partaking of the Body and Blood of Christ, / we may be gathered into one by the Holy Spirit" (RM, 105). Eucharistic Prayer III says even more: "[G]rant that we, who are nourished / by the Body and Blood of your Son / and filled with his Holy Spirit, / may become one body, one spirit in Christ" (RM, 113). At least two effects are revealed here. First, those of us "who are nourished" by Holy Communion become what we eat (as St. Augustine preached in Sermon 272); that is, we become more perfectly members of the Body of Christ. And secondly, we are also "filled with" the Holy Spirit. In sharing the same Body and the same Spirit, we share a bond of unity because we share a bond of identity. We both are and become more perfectly the Body of Christ by the Self-gift of the risen Lord and the power of the Holy Spirit.

Such depth, this mystery of identity, of becoming! But the Beloved does not transform us simply for ourselves. Like the ever Self-giving Son, we are transformed to reach out to others with a gift of Presence and identity. We are called to be faithful to this gift, and to share it for the good of others.

Reflective and Prayerful Interlude

- **When I consider the gifts God offers me at the Eucharistic celebration, I am moved to . . .**
- **I am most open to the work of the Holy Spirit within me when I . . .**
- **The gifts I offer at Mass are . . .**
- **I am dismissed at Mass to live the transforming gift I have received and so . . .**

Transformed to Live the Life of the Beloved

The Eucharist transforms us into persons who share ever more deeply in divine Life and Being; therefore, we are called to live out in our daily lives the Life and identity with which we have been gifted. The Eucharist is a gift with strings attached: we cannot just receive; we also must give.

Celebration of Eucharist, ideally, brings about a transformation in the worshipers. The proclamation of God's Word always challenges us to a greater surrender to take up our baptismal commitment to live the dying and rising mystery of Christ. The Eucharistic Prayer draws us into our Christian story; by hearing God's mighty deeds on our behalf—and especially Jesus' saving life and ministry—we are encouraged, invited, and enabled to participate ritually in redemption. This participation is perhaps best symbolized by Communion, whereby we eat and become sharers in the divine Life, the divine I AM. The transformation is not only of identity—we become more deeply members of the Body of Christ—but is also one of perspective. Because we become God-like, we also assume God's standpoint. Here is perhaps the deepest meaning of our being created images of God: we take on God's perspective, way of being and acting, so we can be and act thus. It is also the deepest meaning of Eucharistic transformation: by being transformed more perfectly into the Body of Christ, we are transformed into relating to each other in the way that God graciously chooses to relate to us (see chapter 14 of John's Gospel, where Jesus speaks of the intimate relationship between him and his Father and between him and us).

God always has concern for the "widow, orphan, and sojourner"—a biblical formulary for anyone without means, family ties, or land; in short, anyone in need—and when we take on God's perspective through Eucharistic transformation, God's concerns become our concerns. Identifying with and serving others is God-like behavior consistent with our gradual transformation into being a Eucharistic people. To share in Eucharist without a concomitant concern for others is to eat and drink to our own condemnation (see 1 Corinthians 11:17–34). It is this simple. It is this demanding.

Yes, living as Jesus lived, being as self-giving as Jesus, makes demands on us. But a curious thing happens: the more like the risen Christ we become, the easier it is to live this life. The easier it is to say yes to helping others, to caring for others, to forgiving others. The more like the risen Christ we become by sharing in the Eucharistic banquet, the more able we are to see Christ in others and reach out to the Beloved who dwells in them. The Eucharist enables us to be more loving and kinder, more merciful and forgiving, more compassionate and just.

Reflective and Prayerful Interlude

- **I become more aware of others and their needs at Eucharist when . . .**
- **Living in the self-giving way Jesus lived means I must . . .**
- **I am aware of becoming more like the risen Christ at Eucharist when I . . .**
- **Eucharist opens to me these new possibilities . . .**

Transformed to Share Already in the Eternal Life of the Beloved

At Eucharist, heaven and earth embrace each other in a holy kiss. At Eucharist an intimacy emerges between heaven and earth, between God and assembly members that it transforms in its power. One new and yet largely undeveloped challenge of the Second Vatican Council through the revision of liturgy is to realize ever more clearly that in "the earthly liturgy we take part in a foretaste of that heavenly liturgy celebrated in the holy city of Jerusalem toward which we journey as pilgrims" (SC, 8). At Eucharist we participate in the heavenly Banquet where we are fulfilled beyond hope, received beyond belief, embraced in a love that is eternal. At Eucharist we are immersed in heaven on earth. At Eucharist we join with all the heavenly choirs in singing "Holy, holy, holy" (RM, 31).

The "Holy, Holy, Holy" concludes the preface of the Eucharistic Prayer, which is the prayer reminding us of God's love for us through creation and salvation. Unlike a preface found in fiction or non-fiction books, which is set apart from the main text, the preface at Mass is an integral part of the Eucharistic Prayer (see "Order of Mass," RM 31). The preface sets the tone for our praying at any given celebration. This "tone" opens us to God's loving faithfulness toward us through the continuation of creation and salvation on our behalf. Nonetheless, because every preface concludes with our singing the "Holy, Holy, Holy," our voices are continually raised to heaven: "[a]nd so, with the Angels and all the Saints / we declare your glory, / as with one voice we acclaim:" (RM, 99); other preface conclusions use similar words. Our localized assembly is really not so small; we celebrate and acclaim in the company of all the angels and saints—past, present, and future.

In the Apostles' Creed we profess belief in "the communion of saints" (RM, 19). It is significant that the two paragraphs in *Lumen gentium* that treat the veneration of the saints (LG, 50, 51) are found in chapter VII, which deals with the eschatological (a term referring to the end times) nature of the Church. *Lumen gentium* underscores the purpose of this veneration as twofold: (1) to inspire us to seek the eschatological reign of God, and (2) to see in the saints a safe path for achieving perfect union with Christ. Then *Lumen gentium* continues its reflection by reminding us that saints have lived successfully both in this time and the next. Companionship with the saints is a bond of love and charity for the community; Eucharist is a concrete means to join the heavenly choir in singing God's praises. So much more is happening at each Mass when we sing "Holy, holy, holy" than we can even imagine!

Discussions of communion with the saints often limit "saint" to those who are officially recognized by the Church, those who are canonized. But when the *Catechism of the Catholic Church* clearly states that "[t]he communion of saints is the Church" (CCC, 946), we are invited to remember that all of us who are united in one Body as the Church are in communion with each other. This is a very comforting and loving thought: the communion of saints includes our deceased loved ones. How wonderful that at each Mass, when we sing "Holy, holy, holy," we are singing with all those who have gone before us and made us who we are!

At Eucharist, we choose the Beloved, who offers the divine Self to us under the appearances of bread and wine, transformed into the Body and Blood of the risen Christ. We eat and drink. We are immersed in the mystery. We are transformed. At Eucharist the waiting is over. The Beloved possesses us. We possess the Beloved.

Reflective and Prayerful Interlude

- I experience heaven and earth embracing each other in a kiss when . . .
- I feel embraced in love at Eucharist when I . . .
- When I sing the "Holy, Holy, Holy" I must . . .
- My loved ones who are present with me at Eucharist are . . .

CHAPTER 4

Self-Giving: Eucharist as Paschal Mystery

The "terrible twos" are no myth, nor are they a joke. The favorite word of a two-year-old? NO! Sometimes young children say no even when they mean yes. It is a natural state in child development. The child has learned to say some words, but has not developed speech enough really to express her or his feelings or needs. The child is beginning to develop independence but in that process learns there are rules that govern choices. Children may throw things out of sheer frustration with everyone and everything around them. They eventually grow out of the terrible twos as they grow physically, intellectually, and emotionally. As St. Paul revealed about himself, "When I was a child, I spoke like a child, I thought like a child, I reasoned like a child" (1 Corinthians 13:11a). But if we want to get along in this world, grow into our full potential, we must "put an end to childish ways" (1 Corinthians 13:11b) and speak, think, and reason like an adult. This development from child to adult is not only true for our human selves; it is equally true for our spiritual selves.

Of course, we do not expect children to have the faith, knowledge, or commitment of adults. We grow into that. In fact, we grow spiritually all our lives. If we do not risk growth, we risk cutting ourselves off from all the good gifts with which God blesses us. Unlike human development, spiritual growth is not obviously linear, passing through various defined stages in an orderly movement. For most of us, growth in our spiritual life progresses through fits and starts. Spiritual directors might talk about the "dark night of the soul," a time of spiritual dryness during which God seems distant, prayer is dry and unsatisfying, and we might feel confused and experience extreme doubt about ourselves, God, and our faith. It is a kind of spiritual "terrible twos" that many of us move through on our journey toward final union with God.

But through all our spiritual growth, one thing is certain, as St. Paul tells us: "Love never ends" (1 Corinthians 13:8a). Love is expressed in many ways. It can be grossly misunderstood or deeply appreciated. When deep love is expressed, it involves the whole being. St. Paul gives us some practical insight about love: "Love is patient; love is kind; love is not envious or boastful or arrogant or rude. It does not insist on its own way; it is not irritable or resentful; it does not rejoice in wrongdoing, but rejoices in the truth. It bears all things, believes all things, endures all things" (1 Corinthians 13:4–7). This is an apt description of how God loves us. What a challenge for how we are to love one another! The key to grasping the connection between Eucharist and the paschal mystery is love—Love that is self-giving.

The Gift of Love

We cannot buy love. We cannot earn love. We do not deserve love. It is a gift from one to another, a gift from lover to the beloved. A two-year-old might scream and stomp her or his little feet in the store trying to convince mommy or daddy to buy a desired toy. We can scream and stomp our feet all we want to receive love, but it does not work that way. Love is a pure gift, and must be both received and given. If love is received but not given, it cannot bear fruit for ourselves or for others. Love is an exchange of our whole selves, freely received and given.

Love is one of the three theological virtues gifted by God to us at baptism (the other two are faith and hope). Since we know that God is love (1 John 4:16b), we know that the most desirable form of love comes from God, and our own human sharing of love is possible only because

God has already showered divine love upon us. Like so many mysteries we meet in our lives, love cannot be easily explained and really, as mystery, love can never be fully realized until we are united eternally with God in heaven. It is not by mere chance that love is so often expressed through art forms, especially poetry and song. Art frees the spirit to soar; love frees the soul to soar.

For all the many descriptions of love there are, one that seems to be rather consistent throughout the whole spectrum of our experiences of love is a drive to unity. This is visible in devoted married love, in enduring friendship love, and in faithful spiritual love. Love advances a drive to closeness with others that reveals the mystery of each other. This is so very true of how God loves us and desires to be in union with us. God is a passionate lover! In the Old Testament, God is portrayed as a jealous lover, one who allows no other gods and pursues Israel even in its infidelity. The gift of God's love is expressed in calling Israel to be God's beloved people, in giving them the land "flowing with milk and honey" (Exodus 3:8b), but especially in calling them out of slavery into freedom. Love frees us to be in union with God and each other.

No greater act of love is possible than the incarnation, life, ministry, death, and resurrection of Jesus Christ. In him God's love is fully revealed as well as Jesus' deep and abiding love for us: "As the Father has loved me, so I have loved you; abide in my love" (John 15:9). Jesus goes on to say in this passage from John's Gospel that we are not slaves, but friends of God, for "[n]o one has greater love than this, to lay down one's life for one's friends" (John 15:13). We hear these Scripture passages about the depth of Jesus' love for us often, but we must hear them with ears finely tuned to Jesus' great longing for us to respond in kind, to the cost of this unfathomable love, to the intimacy this love promises. The gift of divine love for us flows from the very heart of God's Self-love.

While it is true that emotion does not necessarily determine how much or how little we love, at the same time we ought not discount emotion as a window onto the depth of our love. When taken as the sole descriptor of love, or when we love only to have certain emotions well up, then caution is certainly advised. But when emotions are taken as the tangible presence of a love that reflects the lover's desire for only good for the beloved, then emotions can be very positive and affirming.

If indeed, as the creation account in Genesis tells us, we are made in the image of God (see Genesis 1:26), then we are made in divine love. If love is God's being, then love is also our being. If all creation is a self-communication of the divine, and we human beings are the most beloved of God's creation, then we are best served by remembering that our very purpose for living is to love. Love begets life, as is clear in the life-giving love within the Life of the Holy Trinity, and as must be clear in our own daily living. Love begets life only when it is self-giving, only when it is the surrender of self for the good of another without counting the cost.

Reflective and Prayerful Interlude

- **The gifts of love I have received are . . .**
- **I experience love being received and given as a union, as a communion when . . .**
- **God is love, so . . .**
- **I am surprised when my love for others begets love in that . . .**

The Self-Giving of Love

Love is not something we receive in order to keep. No, love must be gifted to another if it is to bear fruit. Love is always for giving. In particular, love is self-giving.

Self-giving has its limits! There are some things about ourselves so deep and private that they could do harm if shared. Any self-giving that puts ourselves or others at physical or spiritual risk is surely not healthy. Self-giving requires a true readiness to receive and give. We must have love before we can give love. Our self-giving must also flow from our own openness to receive from others, and in this way we mature in our spiritual life. We gradually grow into our ability to be self-giving as we faithfully journey toward the fullness of Life. And, of course, Jesus is the perfect model of self-giving. It is helpful spiritually for us to reflect and pray often about how his self-giving life can become a habit of our own living and loving.

The self-giving of love presupposes attentiveness and caring. It presumes an unspoken kind of communication that expresses a close and sometimes intimate relationship. An interesting and telling example of this self-giving of love is the well-known story of the wedding feast at Cana (see John 2:1–12). Mary is attentive to the requirements for the feast and caring toward the comfort of the newlyweds. She notices that the wine is running out. That would surely tend to put a damper on the celebration and embarrass the newlyweds! She makes a simple statement (not a request) to her son Jesus: "They have no wine" (John 2:3b). Jesus seems to answer her in a rather uncaring way, questioning why it is any concern of theirs. But the real issue here lies in what Jesus next says to his mother: "My hour has not yet come" (John 2:4b). In other words, Jesus is saying he is not yet ready to begin his public ministry. Here is an amazing thing about this Gospel passage: Mary seems to be instrumental in inaugurating Jesus' public ministry. She does not answer Jesus directly, but tells the servants, "Do whatever he tells you" (John 2:5). So Jesus performs the first recorded miracle in John's Gospel, his first public act of self-giving love. This brief exchange between Jesus and his mother shows us how deep and intimate their love for each other must have been. Mary is perfectly confident in her relationship with her divine Son and that Jesus will respond. And he does! What a self-giving love exchange!

The amount of water turned into the best wine is staggering. Jesus did not change just a little water into wine, but "six stone water jars . . . each holding twenty or thirty gallons" (John 2:6). That calculates to 120 to 180 gallons of wine! What could have been an embarrassing disaster for the young couple turns into enough wine for a prolonged feast. Just so is the lavish self-giving love that God bestows on each of us. This extravagant divine love we receive in many ways in our daily living is a foreshadowing of the fullness of Life and love we will receive when we pass from this mortal life into eternal Life. God's self-giving love is already a share in the total union with God that we call heaven.

Sometimes self-giving love does not seem to cost anything at all. Spending some time with family and friends simply to be present to each other is enjoyable enough, but it bears much fruit in terms of strengthening relationships. At other times, there can be a steep cost to self-giving love. It cost Jesus his life. He suffered and died on the cross because he was steadfastly resolute in doing the will of his Father, which was to announce a new commandment of love. Because Jesus' preaching and teaching upended some of the Jewish leadership's burdensome laws, he angered them to the point that only demanding his death would satisfy their self-righteousness. Jesus was a threat to them, and they chose to eliminate the threat instead of changing and embracing Jesus' new commandment of love. Their choice was certainly a most unloving act on the part of some of the Jewish leaders. So Jesus died. He gave his all because he loved us so much.

This type of self-giving love is witnessed by many women and men throughout the history of the Church. These martyrs have given their all—their very lives—in fidelity to their love for God and others. Jesus foretold that he would "undergo great suffering, and be rejected by the elders, chief priests, and scribes, and be killed" (Luke 9:22). And he did suffer and die. He also commanded that if "any want to become my followers, let them deny themselves and take up their cross daily and follow me" (Luke 9:23). All of us are called to live the self-giving love for others that Jesus lived, even to the point of death. Self-giving love, then, means surrendering our all, even our very life.

Now, realistically, most of us are not going to become martyrs. If baptism only promised being crucified, probably very few people would choose it! What Jesus is challenging us to accept is that there ought to be no limits to our self-giving love. Jesus laid out the absolute paradigm: love means giving one's all. In reality, our dying to self does not lie in a single instance of being nailed to a cross, but it is a daily saying yes to living the Gospel with fidelity and joy. As a way to show that we desire to grow in our own self-giving love, we accept whatever inconveniences or difficulties come our way. Self-giving love is the persistent surrender of ourselves for the good of others. The story of the wedding feast at Cana encourages us in this kind of love: God gives us a superabundance of the best of blessings—divine Self-giving love—which enriches our lives beyond what we could ever imagine.

Reflective and Prayerful Interlude

- **I am most able to be attentive to the needs of others when I . . .**
- **I experience the depth of God's love for me most often when . . .**
- **In recent days, the cost of my self-giving love has been . . .**
- **Some of God's superabundant blessings to me are . . .**

The Mystery of Love

When little children are asked how much they love mommy or daddy, sometimes they will stretch out their arms as wide as they can and say, "This much!" In their own way they are trying to convey something about the mystery of love they can grasp even at a very young age. The very nature of love is to be extensive and inexhaustible. We ought never say to another that we love her or him totally. To do so could limit our ability to constantly learn something new about the other and could curtail a deeper union we seek with the other. Because love is a mystery, we cannot exhaust it or its possibilities. A mystery can never be completely known. To be certain, something about a mystery can be understood; but even these insights are a very small penetration into the depths we plumb. Our efforts to delve more into the meaning of a mystery spur us on to think ever more deeply about the revelation that a mystery gradually discloses. All we can do is to keep discovering more and more of its riches. The mystery of love impels us to deepen our relationship with another. On the other hand, we can refuse to love. Doing so would be to cut ourselves off from the other. The worst case of choosing not to love another is to refuse to receive God's love and respond with our love. This rejection of love is equivalent to refusing our very life.

No one can live without love because love begets life. The mystery of love is a matter of choosing life. Preserving life is one of the strongest instincts we have. Parallel to this, loving another is an equally strong instinct. Living without love is a life hardly worth living. Therefore, we are relentless in our search for love, in our desire to enter more profoundly into its depth and mystery, in our longing for the sense of wholeness and well-being that the mutual giving and receiving of love bring. In spite of the gripping attraction of love, as humans not all of us are so flourishing in our love lives as we would desire; some have a flawed understanding of love due to unhealthy relationships or lack of family or community. Unrequited love can bring disappointment, hurt, and broken relationships. Not so with divine love. God loves us when we are faithful or unfaithful, when we are attentive or distracted, when we are self-giving or selfish. God's love is never withdrawn. Jesus promised to be with us always. Indeed, the very last words of Matthew's Gospel assure us of this enduring divine Presence: "And remember, I am with you always, to the end of the age" (Matthew 28:20b). This is no empty promise. Jesus' self-giving love is always with us, and in the Eucharist, it is with us in a personal and intimate way. Eucharist is a celebration of Jesus' Self-giving, an enactment in the here-and-now of the mystery of his dying and rising, of his love.

Self-giving love is at the heart of both Eucharist and paschal mystery and unites them as one mystery. Because of this correlation, Eucharist and paschal mystery truly both make known one and the same saving mystery. At each Eucharist Jesus is both victim and priest (a priest is a mediator between God and the people). As *priest* Jesus offers the sacrifice; as *victim* he himself is the offering. Jesus is the Lamb of God (see John 1:29), as John the Baptist declared. He is the memorial sacrifice; he is the One who gives his life for the sake of others. While

Jesus' Self-offering of his human life happened once-and-for all on the cross, this historical event did not signal the end of his Self-offering. By giving himself to us as his very Body and Blood to eat and drink at each Eucharist, Jesus continues to give himself to us always and everywhere. This Self-giving is the memorial of his love. His Self-giving love draws us at each Eucharistic celebration into the mystery of his Self-giving dying and rising. His Self-giving love draws us more deeply into the very mystery of love.

Jesus died because he loves us infinitely. Jesus was raised from the dead because the Father loves him infinitely as the divine Son. Each time we celebrate Eucharist we surrender ourselves to the mystery of divine love. Each time we celebrate Eucharist we surrender ourselves to Jesus' mystery of dying and rising. Every Eucharistic celebration enacts the mystery of divine Self-giving love, the mystery of Jesus' total surrender of himself by dying and rising, the mystery of the invitation for our own participation in this mystery of self-giving love.

It is self-giving that unpacks the one mystery of Eucharist as paschal mystery. Every Eucharist is a celebration of Jesus' self-giving love that began with his incarnation, continued through his ministry, and culminated on the cross and at the resurrection. Jesus' self-giving love continues today in the celebration of the Eucharist. It is here that we are invited to share intimately in this love through eating and drinking his very Body and Blood. Our acceptance of that invitation is a commitment to take up Jesus' self-giving love by dying to ourselves for the sake of others. We rise to new Life by aligning ourselves with Jesus' own commitment to love us "to the very end" (John 13:1c). As we eat and drink at Eucharist and are thus transformed into being more perfect members of the Body of Christ, we assume responsibility for continuing his saving mission; we assume responsibility for loving each other into the fullness of Life. At Eucharist we are already standing in the Presence of God, becoming who God created us to be: one with God for all eternity. With Eucharist as paschal mystery, as self-giving love, the waiting is over. The Beloved possesses us. We possess the Beloved.

Reflective and Prayerful Interlude

- I have received the gift of love in my life from . . .
- God's love impels me to . . .
- I am most comfortable with the demands of self-giving love when . . .
- Eucharist as paschal mystery says to me . . .

CHAPTER 5

A Life for Waiting

It is estimated that we human beings spend about five years (yes, years!) of our lives waiting. We stand and wait in checkout lines, we sit and wait in congested traffic, we frustratingly wait to get a live voice to greet us when we call a customer service center. Let's face it: our daily lives are punctuated with waiting.

Waiting is time we spend inactive until something we want or need happens. Some waiting frustrates us, for example when the kids are dilly-dallying getting ready for school, causing us to be late to work. Some waiting tests our patience, for example when the doctor runs behind schedule and we are a good bit beyond our appointment time. Some waiting irritates us, for example when dinner guests do not come at the appointed time and the meal is getting overcooked.

We wait, we wait, we wait. To what avail? That certainly depends on the kind of waiting we undergo. Some waiting can be for a rather short time, while other waiting can be quite prolonged. Some waiting is unproductive, while other waiting can bear much fruit. We might distinguish two kinds of waiting: waiting that delays us (and so largely is a waste of our valuable time) and waiting that attends to others (and so promotes deepening relationships and spiritual growth).

What Kind of Waiting?

The first kind of waiting, that which delays us, is preferably avoided, but cannot always be. We cannot control how long the checkout line is, but we can make choices about our response. We can look for a shorter line. We can decide to use a self-checkout option that is available with fewer people in line. We can use the waiting time for something productive, like checking our texts or emails on the phone, making out a to do list, or even counting our blessings. We cannot control this kind of waiting, but we can control our responses and choose to make something positive happen during the waiting time.

The second kind of waiting—attending to others—happens all the time, and all too often we simply take it for granted. When we are seated in a restaurant, we presume that a table server will come rather quickly and wait on us, bringing water, handing us menus, explaining specials. When an airplane takes off and reaches a certain altitude, flight attendants come down the aisle with those skinny little carts and offer us something to drink and the proverbial snacks. When we are staying overnight in a hotel or motel, a housekeeping attendant will knock on the door and come in to freshen the room. In all these and many other similar situations, a service is rendered. But really, more happens.

Serving others initiates relationships. In some cases, we might leave a tip to show our appreciation, and the size of the tip indicates how pleased we are with the service. A smile, courtesy, and attentiveness tend to generate the kind of relationship that leaves us with good feelings toward the other. Most of these encounter relationships are temporary; we may never see the table waiter or housekeeper again. On the other hand, our encounter relationships with the Beloved are neither casual nor temporary. Our encounters with the Beloved are lifelong and life-changing. These encounters with the Beloved require a unique kind of waiting on the Beloved: we are called to be attentive to the Beloved, which is a kind of ministering to the Beloved. How so?

After proclaiming the Mystery of Faith at Mass, the presider, when using Eucharistic Prayer II, continues with these intriguing words: "giving thanks that you have held us worthy / to be in your presence and minister to you" (RM, 105). When we think of ministering to another, we think in terms of meeting that other's need. It is much more comfortable to consider ministering to each other than ministering to God. So, what would it mean to "minister" to God, as Eucharistic Prayer II prays? The easy answer is that we minister to God by ministering to our neighbor in whom God resides. That is true, but something far deeper is implied by our Eucharistic praying.

The key to figuring out how we minister to God lies in recognizing and accepting our worth, our dignity. Who we are is a gift from the God who loves us beyond measure. This is the God who created us, who formed us with such loving intent, who called us by name, thus claiming each of us for God's very own (see Isaiah 43:1). God initiated an incredible and personal relationship with every one of us from the very beginning of our lives and at our baptism into Christ. This personal relationship is fostered in sharing Eucharist and every time we acknowledge God's goodness and will in our lives. Our relationship with God never grows old. It is always refreshed and renewed when we minister to God simply by responding to the love relationship God offers us. Our ministering to God is a matter of opening ourselves fully to God's gifts freely given and of accepting the consequences of being in such an extraordinary relationship with our Beloved.

Every relationship has its demands because every relationship is a dynamic movement back and forth from one to another. It is no surprise that the relationship we have with our Beloved does make demands yet leaves us surprisingly free to meet those demands. Our Beloved demands of us a loving response to the divine overtures, which ought to be nothing less than our own entire self-gift to God, who gifts Self so totally to us. We wait on our Beloved when we recognize and surrender ourselves to God's permeating and lasting Presence within us and are willing to share that Presence with others through our own loving and caring. We wait on our Beloved when we express gratitude for the countless divine blessings that are showered upon us. We wait on our Beloved when we are faithful to the love covenant that God has made with each of us.

The kind of waiting on our Beloved that draws us out of the mundane and into Life-giving divine Presence is nothing less than our willingness to keep God at the center of our lives by being attentive to God's overtures of divine Presence. This does not mean that we are thinking of God during every one of our waking moments. This is not really possible and certainly not practical if we hope to do what we must to meet family needs, to put a roof over our heads and food on the table. Our everyday lives do demand our full attention most of the time. Rather, we keep God at the center of our lives when we form the good habits that help us make simple, everyday choices that reflect our commitment to doing God's will, which is a reflection of the loving relationship we have chosen to have with our Beloved and our desire to be attentive to God's desires for us. We witness to God being the center of our lives when our faces radiate with the joy, light, and love that come from deep within, where we are in touch with God's Presence. People notice. How others respond to us reveals how well we keep God at the center of our lives.

Our waiting on our Beloved is the kind of waiting that draws us to an ever-greater attentiveness to the God who dwells within us. God is always present; we need never wait for God to come to us. The work of waiting rests on our shoulders. Our wistful cries are to wake us up to that loving Presence: "I wait for the Lord, / my soul waits, / and in his word I hope; / my soul waits for the Lord" (Psalm 130:5–6a). God's Word brings hope because the divine Word awakens in us the expectation that not only is God ever present, but we have been gifted with the ability to respond and bask in that Presence of our Beloved. Our waiting on our Beloved arouses a deep longing: "My soul longs, indeed it faints / for the courts of the Lord; / my heart and my flesh sing for joy / to the living God" (Psalm 84:2).

Reflective and Prayerful Interlude

- **Waiting is a positive and fruitful experience for me when I . . .**
- **I can increase my attentiveness to others if I would . . . to God if I would . . .**
- **Waiting on God wells up gratitude in me because . . .**
- **Waiting on my Beloved means to me . . . helps me to . . .**

Waiting as Longing for the Beloved

As we reflect on waiting on our Beloved, obviously we are not wasting time. Far from it! Waiting on our Beloved is a fruitful time of growth, grace, and gratitude. It is a time of growth because any attentiveness to God conditions our attentiveness to others. It is a time of grace because any attentiveness to God increases our capacity for God's Life to dwell within us. It is a time of gratitude because any attentiveness to God wells up in us a realization of how gifted and blessed we are. All this is good; all this deepens our prayer and spiritual life in such a way that the lures and cares of this world diminish with our increasing attentiveness to God's Presence, and all this opens us to the wonder and surprise that await us in the world to come. Nevertheless, as pleasing as the growth, grace, and gratitude are, waiting wells up something else in us: an ingrained longing for the Beloved.

Longing is a burning desire for someone or something; it can include a sense of need. Often, we long for material things, such as the latest iPhone or SUV. Desiring and acquiring the things of this world simply leave us longing for yet more; this longing confuses *want* with *need*. Longing for things seldom leaves us satisfied; there is always something more and better. It can leave us quite agitated, discontented, and striving for all the wrong things in life that we think will make us happy. And they never do.

Longing for someone can be stifling and selfish, or it can be wholesome and holy. The former seeks one's own good instead of the good of the other. Often this longing ends in broken relationships simply because the longing is not life-giving for the other (and ultimately is not life-giving for the one who is longing, either). A wholesome and holy longing leads to sincere effort to be with the other in a reciprocal relationship of shared goodness.

Some relationships prove to be temporary. Seldom do friends we make early in life continue to be part of our daily lives, especially as we move on to get an education, marry and begin a family, or advance in the workplace. Often, we do not even see our blood relatives as frequently as when we were growing up, and we perhaps even lose track of them altogether. Other relationships, however, prove to be ongoing. They include the people who are willingly present to us, those on whom we can depend for help or a listening ear when we need it, and those for whom the love that is shared is life-giving.

Longing is certainly wholesome and holy when we turn our longing toward the Beloved. We can never long enough for the Beloved. Longing for the divine One turns us toward what is most permanent: the eternal God, who ceaselessly desires good for us. Our longing for God is, ultimately, an intense longing to be united in the communion of the Holy Trinity for all eternity. This longing increases as we raise our hearts in hope toward the Beloved.

Hope is the virtue that enables expectation to become reality, that invites us to reach for possibilities beyond our imagination, and that assures us that the daily journey toward eternal Life with our Beloved is growing toward our desired union. Without hope, any longing we have for our Beloved would not be fulfilled. St. Paul reminds us of the value of hope: "For in hope we were saved. Now hope that is seen is not hope. For who hopes for what is seen? But if we hope for what we do not see, we wait for it with patience" (Romans 8:24). The "unseen" for which we hope is eternal Life. Longing tempers our impatience with waiting.

Hope is a kind of hospitality for the Beloved. Hospitality is being at home with another or others. Hospitable hostesses or hosts make their guests feel at home by warmly welcoming them, showing them to comfortable seating, offering refreshments, engaging in mutually interesting conversation, and paying attention to them. We are hospitable toward our Beloved when we welcome God into our heart and spirit in such a way that we ourselves are the tabernacle-home for God's Presence. This hospitable welcoming plays out in opening ourselves to the Beloved such that we are able to receive the divine Word about who we are and how we are to live. Our hope is not a temporary wish, but a desire for the eternal Beloved.

Waiting as longing for the Beloved instills a pervasive desire to be present to the Divine. While Christian hope does direct us to the finality of our being, which is eternal Life, it likewise directs us to long for what is at hand: the risen Christ's Self-gift to us in the Eucharistic Presence. Our longing for the Beloved leads us more surely to participate in the Eucharistic celebration with ever greater intent, knowing that at Eucharist we encounter the Beloved in the Word proclaimed and in the very Food and Drink—the true Body and Blood of Christ—that is so generously given. The more we long for our Beloved, the greater will be our focused presence toward the real Presence of the risen Christ.

A life of waiting entails attentiveness to the many ways God is already present, and the anticipation of a fullness of Presence that we can only fleetingly experience on this side of mortal death. A life of waiting draws us to receive Eucharist as a pledge of things already present in addition to a Life that is to come. A life of waiting encourages us to align ourselves with the risen Christ such that our Gospel living is fruitful for both ourselves and others. A life of waiting is a life worth living, because it leads to a hospitality of self that welcomes divine Presence in both expected and unexpected ways. A life of waiting is a life filled with the wonderful and Life-giving surprises of our Beloved.

Reflective and Prayerful Interlude

- **I intensely long for my Beloved in these ways . . .**
- **Longing for my beloved instills in me a desire to . . .**
- **I offer my hospitality to . . .
it helps me to . . .**
- **Longing increases my attentiveness, and so . . .**

Waiting as Lifelong Transformation

All too many people dislike change. They are afraid of the unknown. They are stuck in their own routines, relationships, and scheduled life. When change comes along, in any dimension of their lives, they often become agitated, frustrated, unglued. Some people refuse to change, and their lives are poorer for it. Change opens a door onto growth. Transformation is a kind of change that opens a door onto becoming someone more than we are. To embrace transformation as a way of living is to choose lifelong growth that is an unending process of becoming. In this unending becoming, we grow ever closer to our final union with God and the fullness of divine Life that is promised us.

Daily living always makes demands on us, whether those demands are for time spent doing for others, learning a skill to advance in the workplace, or simply getting dinner on the table on time for the family. Some demands are routine and not all that consequential. Other demands are of great consequence. St. Paul reminds us: "Do not be conformed to this world, but be transformed by the renewing of your minds, so that you may discern what is the will of God—what is good and acceptable and perfect" (Romans 12:2). This consequential transformation is nothing less than the requirement of baptism: that the old self must die in order to rise in new Life in Christ. This new Life continually transforms us into more than we are as we grow into the Beloved.

We are daily being transformed into the new Life that we will enjoy fully in eternity.

Waiting as lifelong transformation implies a developing attentiveness to the Beloved. It prods us to seek God's will and be faithful in carrying it out, for doing God's will in a "good and acceptable and perfect" (Romans 12:2) way is what Jesus came to teach us as the sure way to his Father. Jesus said, "I can do nothing on my own. . . . I seek to do not my own will but the will of him who sent me" (John 5:30). Jesus himself is the way to his Father; when we, too, do God's will, then we align ourselves with our Beloved on the way to that perfect union for which we long.

We learn God's will by hearing and heeding Jesus' words. The Good News Jesus taught shapes our lives so we walk the way of Jesus. The way of Jesus is a road of self-giving, of mercy and compassion, of willing the good of others no matter the cost to us. This way is not always an easy way, as the Gospels tell us. Jesus faced misunderstanding and ridicule, and the cross of denial and betrayal was surely heavy. But Jesus never swerved from the message of salvation he came to share with us. When we hear the Gospel challenge to walk in Jesus' very own footsteps, we must wait on the Beloved—encounter the Beloved—if we are to be strong and courageous in taking up our own daily cross to follow Jesus. We must die to ourselves, even lose our own lives: "Jesus told his disciples, 'If any want to become my followers, let them deny themselves and take up their cross and follow me. For those who want to save their life will lose it, and those who lose their life for my sake will find it'" (Matthew 16:24–25). But this loss of our own lives is not really a great loss; rather, it is a great gain. The life we lose is choosing to do our own selfish will, which only brings untold emptiness. The life we gain is the very Life of God given when we do God's will, a gift to us who are beloved of God. This Life we gain only brings transforming fullness.

God does not abandon us to our own limiting strategies to follow the divine will. Jesus was sent to show us the way to God and how to do God's will faithfully. The Word Made Flesh is still with us to teach us and guide us. Waiting as lifelong transformation takes into account the multiple ways we encounter the risen Christ who is still present to us and teaching us. His own life eloquently teaches us how to die to self in order to rise to new Life; we need only read the Sacred Scriptures to discover how we do this and be immersed in the depth of his love for us. We listen to Scripture proclaimed each time we celebrate Mass and then are nourished to live that Word by the risen Christ's very own Body and Blood. Eucharist as paschal mystery is a synopsis of our daily Gospel living. With all Gospel living, the waiting is over. The Beloved possesses us. We possess the Beloved.

Reflective and Prayerful Interlude

- **I resist change when I . . .**
- **I accept change and am transformed to . . .**
- **The will of God for me right now is to . . .**
- **Following Jesus' way of life delights me when I . . .**
- **Hearing words as the Word of the Beloved helps me to . . .**

CHAPTER 6

A Life for Intimate Union

It would take a calloused heart, indeed, to look at a tiny baby and not want to pick the infant up and cuddle, kiss, and caress the little one. There is something about the vulnerability, dependence on others, and innocence of young life that is very difficult to resist. Babies naturally bring out the tenderness in us and our inborn need to express and receive warmth and closeness. We are born into a life with a need for intimate union.

Intimacy can have many expressions and meanings. It might be physical, psychological, emotional, or spiritual. Or some combination of all of them. Intimacy assumes connection, a meeting of hearts, minds, souls, and spirits. It points toward a life of belonging together, a choice to be one with another. Intimacy is fulfilling; it instills in us wonder and expectation, joy and delight, a desire for deeper connection and belonging. Intimacy can be enduring only if there is mutual trust, self-disclosure, and an ongoing drive toward understanding and acceptance of the other.

Enduring intimacy unfolds in a community, a network of relationships. Without the care and support of others that draw us out of ourselves into mutual self-giving, intimacy can quickly deteriorate into selfishness, which seriously hampers any growth in love. The nemeses of intimacy are isolation and loneliness. If we cannot reach out beyond ourselves, we cannot be in relationship with others. We might think of our network of relationships as a series of concentric circles. At the center are located our closest relationships, usually family and select friends. As we move farther and farther from the center, our relationships become more casual and less life-giving but are still very much a part of a fulfilling life. Even our casual relationships enhance our lives in such a way that our intimacy with those closest to us grows.

Intimate relationships build over time. It takes time and effort to get to know another in such a way that the relationship grows to a desire for intimate union. This is true of our relationship with God, our Beloved. As we learn how to love others, we learn how to love God. As we learn how to have a strong community with others, so do we learn to have a stronger unity with God. So much about our everyday lives contributes to intimate union with God and others. We need to risk vulnerability. We need to surrender ourselves to trust. We need to give ourselves in love. A life pursuing intimate union is a life stretching for the beloved and the Beloved.

Meal as Intimate Union

"Over the River and Through the Wood" is a familiar Thanksgiving poem by Lydia Maria Child that many learn to sing as children. It brings to mind that holidays are meant for family time. Can one imagine a holiday celebration (or any celebration whatsoever) without food, family, and friends? And often the food is a given. Thanksgiving without turkey, dressing, and cranberries? Impossible! Christmas without ham and green bean casserole? Impossible! Easter without Easter eggs? Impossible! The shared food lends tradition to the shared meal, and tradition implies community.

There is nothing worse than a holiday spent alone, and yet this is a reality for many. Churches and other caring groups sponsor holiday meals to ease the discomfort of the lonely, displaced, and anyone in need. These gatherings build community and foster connections. Meals are social events. The food and drink provide the sustenance, but the people provide the heart, the community, the intimate union. Without others, meals can be simply a biological act of providing the body with nourishment; with others, meals are a time of communion. The sharing community lends a kind of intimacy to the shared meal.

Luke's Gospel has Jesus eating meals with others a lot. His Gospel records six meals during Jesus' teaching ministry, the Last Supper, and two post-resurrection meals, for nine meal accounts altogether. The six meals during Jesus' public ministry are not without their tension and challenges. In each case Jesus is tested about something. Even at the Last Supper there is heartache, predicting Judas' betrayal and Peter's denial. The meals are an occasion for Jesus to reveal further who he is and the mission on which he was sent. The controversy is not for its own sake but becomes a teaching moment to move the hearers further along the path of life Jesus has come to reveal. One particularly interesting meal is revealed in the playfully delightful account of Zacchaeus and Jesus (Luke 19:1–10).

Zacchaeus was not only a hated tax collector, but a chief tax collector. He got rich at others' expense. Obviously, he would hardly have been popular person in the community. He wanted to "see who Jesus was" (19:3a). He made the first overture and went to extremes to see Jesus; being of short stature in the midst of a large crowd, he climbed a sycamore tree. His desire to see Jesus was stronger than his concern about his dignity, stature in the community, or decorum. Zacchaeus was determined to see Jesus. Little did he guess what would happen. As Jesus passed by, "he looked up" (19:5a), saw Zacchaeus, and then Jesus invited himself to the tax collector's house. In other meal accounts, the host invites Jesus; in this account, Jesus invited himself. Luke tells us that Zacchaeus "was happy to welcome him" (19:6). Though Luke does not record an actual meal with Jesus as a guest there no doubt would have been food served and shared. The conversation and hospitable time unfolding between Jesus and Zacchaeus clearly changed the tax collector; instead of extorting people, he gave back to people (19:8). To bring about that kind of rapid change in another, an intimate union no doubt took place. Jesus was at home with Zacchaeus, who in a whole new way became at home with the divine Savior.

Jesus invites himself to be our guest, as he did with Zacchaeus. He desires to be at home with us: in our hearts and lives. We must be as welcoming as Zacchaeus. And just as Zacchaeus' encounter with Jesus changed the tax collector, so will it change us if we listen to the Guest who dwells within. We need not climb a tree for Jesus to invite himself into our heart-homes as our guest; he is always present, awaiting our response. Our Beloved is at home with us, patient until we become attentive enough to wait on our Beloved.

The most important meal to which the risen Christ invites us is the Eucharistic Banquet, where he is the Host and we are his guests. He welcomes us and invites us to change. At Mass we encounter him in exceptional ways. In the Introductory Rites we are showered with his unfailing mercy and forgiveness. No wonder on Sundays and feast days the liturgy calls us to sing the Glory to God in the highest. How can our hearts not rise up in praise in face of such divine love and compassion? We encounter the risen Christ in the proclaimed Gospel when we are his disciples learning his path to Life. We are challenged in this Word-encounter to change, as Jesus changed Zacchaeus. We encounter him in the universal prayer (prayer of the faithful) when we confidently make known our needs. We know that he knows what is best for us and will answer our prayers. We encounter him as the gifts of bread and wine are placed on the altar, and we place ourselves on the altar. We ourselves are offered up with them, surrendering ourselves to God's marvelous transforming action. We encounter him in the Eucharistic Prayer, where these humble gifts and we ourselves are consecrated. We eat and drink at Communion and become more perfectly who the risen Christ desires of us: intimately united with him in his Body. We encounter him in the final blessing, when we are reminded of our holiness and then sent forth to be the risen Presence of Christ for others.

The Food of the Eucharistic Banquet lends tradition to the shared meal, and tradition implies community. We eat and drink no ordinary food, but the Divine Host himself. We eat and drink the Body and Blood of the risen Christ, and in that meal share an unequaled intimate union. This Food makes us one in body and spirit with the Divine Host. And it makes us one with all members of the Body of Christ. Celebrating this Meal and eating this Food constitute participation in community as intimate union.

Reflective and Prayerful Interlude

- **Meal traditions I observe and love are . . .**
- **They bring me closer to . . .**
- **I have gone out of my way to encounter Jesus in these ways . . .**
- **I welcome Jesus as my heart-Guest when I . . .**
- **Times I share an unequaled intimate union with the risen Christ are . . .**

Community as Intimate Union

In early 2020, when the coronavirus hit the United States with a vengeance, people's lives were turned upside down. Day after day news programs showed people who died with only a nurse by their bedside to hold their hand. The hospital personnel would use cell phones to connect dying people with their loved ones so they could say their final goodbyes. It was heart-wrenching to know people were dying alone, physically cut off from loved ones. Parents told of how lonely their children were when schools closed and they no longer had contact with their friends. No more play days, and they could not understand why. This was also heart-wrenching. We human beings are social beings by nature. We are born into the family community and then connect with other communities throughout our lives.

When God created Adam, God said, "It is not good that the man should be alone; I will make him a helper as his partner" (Genesis 2:18). What is even more beautiful, Adam and Eve were closely connected to God, in perhaps the very first community. It was a community of intimacy, for God would walk with them "in the garden at the time of the evening breeze" (Genesis 3:8a). How we long for that kind of a friendly walk and chat with God! But the intimate union of their community was soon broken, for Adam and Eve sinned and then "hid themselves from the presence of the LORD God" (Genesis 3:8b). This is heart-wrenching! It was not God who withdrew, but Adam and Eve. We ourselves choose whether we want to be in community with each other and God. We choose whether we want to withdraw or be in intimate union.

One of the most important communities we choose is the community that is the Church. We usually encounter the Church community in our local parishes, particularly when we gather for the celebration of liturgy. Some families have lived in the same parish community for generations; this community has become a true family in the faith. It is here that they experience strong bonds of charity, receive help and care when they need it, and enjoy all the gifts of the Holy Spirit needed to build up the community into full stature as the Body of Christ (see, for example, 1 Corinthians 12:7 and Ephesians 4:11–13). The Acts of the Apostles portrays a beautiful picture of the early Church community and how they related to each other: "Now the whole group of those who believed were of one heart and one soul, and no one claimed private ownership of any possessions, but everything they owned was held in common" (Acts 4:32; see also Acts 2:42–47). To be of "one heart and one soul" requires a shared and intimate communion.

As parishes in some areas have grown larger and larger, with many churches now seating more than a thousand assembly members, it is challenging to get to know others with whom we worship and with whom we are united in Christ. In this day and age, it hardly seems possible that even small Christian communities can hold things in common. Though sharing goods and other external manifestations of community are important, and parishes generously support many good causes, another bond of the Christian community is even more important: the bond of common identity.

The intimate union distinctive of the Christian community rests in its shared identity, shared Food, and shared mission. We are bound together by a spiritual union even stronger than any human bonds. We are bound together by the risen Christ, the Head of the Church, and the Holy Spirit sent to dwell within us. "Blood runs thicker than water" is an English proverb that dates back many centuries. Different interpretations have been proposed over the centuries, but the most common one suggests that blood relatives form our closest bonds. Yet in Christ we have an even closer bond. Jesus gave us his Body and Blood as a memorial of the paschal mystery and as our nourishment for the journey to eternal Life. When we eat and drink this heavenly Food, the Lifeblood coursing through us unites us with Christ and each other in an intimacy that is beyond anything we can effect ourselves.

To convey the depth of this mystery of our intimate union with Christ and each other, Jesus used the metaphor of the vine and branches: "Abide in me as I abide in you. Just as the branch cannot bear fruit by itself unless it abides in the vine, neither can you unless you abide in me. I am the vine, you are the branches" (John 15:4–5a). The branches take their nourishment from the vine; without the vine's sap, the branches dry out and die. We take our Life-giving nourishment from the Self-gift of the risen Christ at Mass. The Holy Spirit effects in us "communion with Christ . . . so to form his Body. The Holy Spirit is like the sap of the Father's vine which bears fruit on its branches" (CCC, 1108; cf. Jn 15:1–7; Gal 5:22). Our bonds in the Body of Christ enable the most intimate union in community that is possible, a union that joins us together in his Body because we are one with the risen Christ.

Our intimate union with the risen Christ touches every aspect of our being and lives, not only in our relationship with Christ but also with each other. The Body of Christ is a real community of persons with like minds and hearts. Like every community, our community as the Body of Christ must continually grow. We must strongly desire and diligently seek this intimate union. We must long for and cherish it. God offers us every help we need to grow in our love for God and each other. Our Beloved never quits on us. Neither can we afford to turn from God if we want to grow in love of our Beloved. Prayer turns us toward our Beloved and draws us to our Beloved. Prayer is an intimate encounter with our Beloved.

Reflective and Prayerful Interlude

- **The communities with which I identify are . . .**
- **Community challenges me most when . . .**
- **It satisfies me most when . . .**
- **I wish my parish community would . . .**
- **I feel intimacy with Christ in the Body of Christ most easily when . . .**

Prayer as Intimate Union

Who among us has not known people who simply radiate joy, peace, happiness, love, kindness? They are people to whom we naturally gravitate. Their goodness rubs off on us. We want to be near them because just being with them makes us better people. These often are also people of deep faith who undoubtedly love their God. As we spend time with them and get to know them, we also discover that they are people with a rich prayer life. Their whole being witnesses to a life of prayer that voices itself by a gentle, quiet presence.

People usually do not speak easily about their prayer life unless some circumstances spark sharing. Yet prayer is nothing less than enjoying intimate union with our Beloved. It is basking in the Presence of our Beloved, anywhere and everywhere. It is a mystery of encounter and communion. Prayer draws us into the very heart of the relationship we grow into with our Beloved on our journey to final union. Prayer gains for us an entry point into identifying with Jesus' saving mystery of dying and rising. "This mystery [of our faith], then, requires that the faithful believe in it, that they celebrate it, and that they live from it in a vital and personal relationship with the living and true God. This relationship is prayer" (CCC, 2558).

About the Author

Joyce Ann Zimmerman, CPPS, PHD, STD, is the director of the Institute for Liturgical Ministry in Dayton, Ohio. She has been a member of the Sisters of the Precious Blood for more than fifty years and worked tirelessly in the liturgical apostolate as a teacher, liturgical consultant, author, mentor, and frequent speaker and facilitator of workshops on liturgy and spirituality. Her publications include *Silence: Everyday Living and Praying, How Deep the Mystery: Meditating on the Words of the Mass, Living a Liturgical Spirituality: Journeying Daily with Christ* (Liturgy Training Publications), and *Worship with Gladness: Understanding Worship from the Heart* (Calvin Institute of Christian Worship).

About the Artist

Linda McCray, MFA, is a visual artist whose studio is nestled in the solitude of the Rocky Mountains of Montana. McCray's boundary-transcending abstract spiritual paintings have been exhibited in the United States and England; published in Belgium, Germany, Canada, and the United States; and are in public and private collections. As an adjunct professor of art, she taught for Loyola University–Chicago, The University of Mary, Helena College: The University of Montana, and Carroll College. She has lectured at art museums, universities, and conferences; written articles for national magazines; served as art consultant; and been an artist-in-residence at the Holter Museum of Art and Blessed Trinity Catholic Community. She graduated *cum laude* from Washington State University with a BA in fine arts, the University of Montana with an MFA in painting and drawing, and Benet Hill Monastery with a certificate in spiritual direction.